Garboldisham is an attractive village, lying hidden away from the Thetford to Diss road, but the sign stands on this road at the road junction. At the top of the post with its finely carved motifs is a model of the post mill, a feature of the village, now restored to use.

EAST ANGLIAN
VILLAGE AND TOWN SIGNS

Ursula Bourne

Shire Publications Ltd

CONTENTS

British Library Cataloguing in Publication data available.

Set in 9 point Times roman and printed in Great Britain by C. I. Thomas & Sons (Haverfordwest) Ltd, Press Buildings, Merlins Bridge, Haverfordwest, Dyfed.

NOTE

At the time when this book was being prepared the signs at the six villages on the Sandringham estate had been removed for renovation. Their positions in the villages have therefore not been given, in case any of them are re-erected at a different spot.

COVER: **Redgrave** village is in Suffolk, a few miles west of Diss, and its carved and painted sign, erected in 1983, stands on the village green, known as the Knoll. On one side, with the fourteenth-century church, the old barn, now converted into cottages, and the windmill, destroyed by fire in 1924, the monks are a reminder that the Abbot of Bury was lord of the manor, and the organ commemorates the Hart family, local organ builders, who built an organ for Mendelssohn. The other side depicts Redgrave Fen — old peat cuttings — and the very rare raft spider which is to be found there. The boar surmounting the sign is the crest of the Bacon family; Sir Nicolas Bacon, Lord Keeper to Elizabeth I, built the old Redgrave Hall.

North Repps, a small village a few miles south of Cromer, possesses a very fine carved and painted sign which stands high in a prominent position at the meeting of several roads. On it are eleven items associated with the parish or with persons who have lived in it.

Flitcham. St Felix of Burgundy, who founded the Christian church in Norfolk, is said to have sailed up the Babingley river to start his evangelical mission in the village of Flitcham. He is seen on the sign, holding his crook, in the stern of a ship.

INTRODUCTION

Village signs, which should not be confused with inn signs, are a feature of the East Anglian countryside. They can be found in other parts of Britain, but the number in East Anglia far exceeds that anywhere else, Norfolk alone having over three hundred. This book includes a good selection of them.

Kind Edward VII had the original idea that, to encourage appreciation of and interest in their villages, the inhabitants should erect village signs, and this was continued by his son George V and grandson George VI. The first signs were erected in the villages on the Sandringham estate and were made in what is now known as the Queen's Carving School.

In 1929 the enterprise received an important stimulus from Harry Carter, a nephew of the renowned Egyptologist Howard Carter, excavator of Tutankhamun's tomb. Born in London and trained at the Slade College of Art, Harry Carter became the arts and technical crafts master of Hamonds Grammar School in the Norfolk town of Swaffham. He became interested in the village sign venture and in 1929 made his first sign, which was erected in Swaffham. Harry Carter afterwards made a great number of signs throughout East Anglia, and even further afield, before his death. His signs are so distinctive that they can be easily identified. They are all carved in wood and brightly painted. His work was meticulous in every detail. A great deal of thought and study went into each sign, which might take him between six months and a year to complete.

One of his problems was obtaining the right wood. It had to be properly seasoned, and though he believed English oak, because of its strength and durability, was the best, he had sometimes to use other woods, such as mahogany or walnut. After painting, the signs were varnished. Instead of gold paint he preferred to use gold leaf because, although it was more expensive, it stood up better to the weather.

Deterioration through exposure to the weather has always been a problem with signs and to keep them in perfect condition they need an occasional refurbishing. Unfortunately, a beautifully executed sign may be neglected, and the colours may become faded and dim. Various devices have been used to protect a sign. One is the provision of a small roof over it, as for example at Drinkstone. Another is to encase a painted sign in a frame with a sheet of glass over it; but unfortunately this does not always provide sufficient protection.

Carved and painted signs similar to Harry Carter's are to be found in many villages, often the work of local artists and craftsmen. There are also some beautiful, though less conspicuous, carved signs which are unpainted — one being the statue of a falconer in Earl Soham. Pictures on plain board, in the style of the usual inn sign, are fairly common, but the sign at Middleton, made in mosaic by a local artist, is probably unique.

A different type of sign, found particularly in Suffolk villages, is that made of wrought iron. These, often the work of a local blacksmith, may be either black or brightly coloured, and many are very striking, standing out sharply against the sky. A good example is the decorative and brightly painted one at Kenninghall. A highly original metal sign is that at Stibbard, constructed of farm implements and metal bits and pieces.

Signs are usually fixed on a post, and the base is often made of a local stone.

The occasion for the erection of a sign is often the commemoration of a centenary or of an event such as the Queen's Silver Jubilee in 1977, when a large number of signs were erected. Those responsible may be the village community as a whole, a private donor or, frequently, the local Women's Institute.

The subject of a sign may be a landmark of the village or town, a local product, craft or industry, a legend or an event in its history, or simply a play on the name.

The siting of signs varies. Where there is a village green or grassy triangle, the sign is often placed in a conspicuous position there. In other cases it may be in a commanding position at the entrance to the village. This may necessitate two signs, one at either end, unless, as at Walberswick, which is bounded on one side by the sea and on another by the river, there is only one main road by which the village can be entered.

Some people regard East Anglia as including not only Norfolk and Suffolk but also parts of Cambridgeshire and north Essex, but in this book only the counties of Norfolk and Suffolk are included.

The signs are most attractive features of their town or village and they could even form the basis for a holiday in the region, or for a day's outing. In this book they have therefore been arranged according to area, starting from the villages on the Sandringham estate in north-west Norfolk, where they originated.

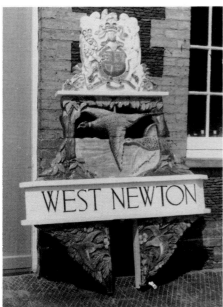

West Newton is the nearest village to Sandringham. The present sign was designed and made by Harry Carter and presented to the Queen in 1955 as a gift from Hamonds Grammar School in Swaffham. Below a carving of the royal arms is a typical local scene with a pair of pheasants in flight and on the two brackets are carvings of two more birds, as well as flowers, fruit and leaves.

Shernborne. The village sign was originally commissioned by King Edward VII when he was still Prince of Wales but has since undergone several alterations in detail. The two figures represent Sir Thomas Shernborne and his wife Jamona, to whom there are bronzes, dated 1438, in the church.

Anmer was once a Roman encampment on the Peddars Way and the figure of a Roman soldier is shown on one of the two sides of the sign. On the other is a boy scout, recording that the sign was the gift of the Boy Scouts of Norfolk to the Queen, in gratitude for her interest in the movement.

Babingley also has a sign (not illustrated) depicting St Felix. According to legend he was shipwrecked on his voyage to Britain and saved by a family of beavers; in return he made the father beaver a bishop. The sign shows St Felix with a ship in the background and, above, the beaver family, with the father in a red robe and mitre, holding a crook.

5

King's Lynn at one time had three signs: one near the river, but this is no longer there; another on the Gayton road leading into the town from north Norfolk; and a third, shown here, by the Hardwick road near the dual carriageway. This is two-sided. On one side appears St Margaret, to whom one of the town's churches is dedicated, and who is reputed to have slain a dragon with her spear; and on the other Henry Bell stands before the Lynn Custom House, of which he was the architect.

Watlington lies a few miles south of King's Lynn. The sign stands at a road junction in the village, opposite the Angel. It depicts the distribution of loaves of bread under an eighteenth-century charity by which twelve loaves of bread are given on alternative Sundays to poor widows of Watlington and the neighbouring village of Tottenhall.

Wolferton. The sign illustrates the Norse legend of the giant wolf Fenrir, who, to show his strength in breaking bonds, consented to be bound if the god Tyr would put his right hand in his mouth; but the bonds proved unbreakable and so Tyr lost his hand.

East Winch, a village a few miles south-east of King's Lynn, combined with its neighbour West Bilney to produce one of the loveliest of all village signs. It stands just off the main road beside the nature reserve of the Norfolk Naturalist Trust and shows the wildlife of the district, with the churches of the two villages in the background.

North Runcton is a village south-east of King's Lynn. Its early eighteenth-century church, built of the local carr-stone, is attributed to Henry Bell, who built the Custom House in King's Lynn. The sign stands at the corner of the green by the church. It shows the church with Henry Bell standing at one side, and below are the arms of the Gurney family, long associated with the village.

Heacham, a village a few miles south of Hunstanton, possesses a most attractive sign. This stands on the main road at the turning opposite the Norfolk Lavender fields. Princess Pocahontas, the daughter of a Red Indian chief, married a Heacham man, John Rolfe. She came to England and was presented at court; on the sign she is portrayed in the court dress of the period. She is supported by two horses, one a 'sea-horse' to mark Heacham's links with the sea, and the other recalling a hackney breed for which the village was famous. Below, with a starfish, is a bunch of lavender, symbolising the Norfolk Lavender products for which Heacham is now famous.

Snettisham is on the main road from King's Lynn to Hunstanton, and the sign is on the left side on entering, just before the hump-backed bridge. It is a striking sign, for it is surmounted by a golden torque, a representation of one found in a nearby field. This is supported by two sea-horses, and beside them are two smugglers and, in the distance, a square-rigged smugglers' craft, a reminder that smugglers once frequented this part of the coast.

Hunstanton, a seaside resort overlooking the Wash, is the only resort in East Anglia which faces west. Its sign, which stands on the large central green on the sea front, shows the sun setting over the sea. The figures are those of St Edmund and the wolf which, according to legend, guarded his head after he had been beheaded by the Danes. There is a cliff named St Edmund's Point, and local legend has it that St Edmund landed here on his way to be crowned king of East Anglia.

Brancaster, on the north Norfolk coast, is the *Branodunum* of Roman times, but today it is a holiday centre, with many new houses, and there are few remains of the Roman fort, which stood between the village and the Staithe. But the Staithe still maintains its connections with the sea, as the village sign shows, for here is the head of a Roman soldier flanked by sea-horses. The sign is on the main road from Wells to Hunstanton, almost opposite the church.

Swaffham. The two-sided sign stands on one side of the market place and was the first to be made by Harry Carter — in 1929. It shows the fifteenth-century pedlar John Chapman, with his dog and a crock of gold. According to the story, Chapman dreamt that if he went to London Bridge he would hear something to his advantage. He went, with his dog, and met a man who told him that he had dreamt that if he went to Swaffham and dug under an apple tree in the garden of a pedlar he would find a crock of gold. The pedlar hastened home and dug under his apple tree and found not one but two crocks of gold. Becoming a wealthy man, he gave money for the building of a new north aisle to the church.

Castle Acre lies a few miles north of Swaffham. The ruined priory is worthy of a visit, as is the village, built in the outer bailey of the ruined castle. The sign, standing in the village centre, shows a reconstruction of the original priory, built by William de Warenne, a follower of William the Conqueror, and, below, a monk of the Cluniac order, for which the priory was built.

Shouldham village, midway between Swaffham and Downham Market, was once a market town and the site of a priory. The sign, which stands on one side of the green, shows, against a background of the priory ruins, a monk and a drover with his animals on the way to market. The well on the shield below represents the Silver Well, a source of a natural mineral water near the village.

Marham, to the west of Swaffham, once had a Cistercian nunnery but is best known today for the Royal Air Force station situated in the parish. The sign, standing by the church, was given to the village on the occasion of the Queen's Silver Jubilee by the RAF to show their appreciation of its hospitality. A Cistercian nun stands in the centre and the side panels show the local pumping station, a plough representing agriculture, an aeroplane of earlier design symbolic of the role of RAF Marham in two world wars, and a bunch of cherries reminiscent of the time when the village was known as Cherry Marham because of the abundance and excellence of the cherries grown there.

Feltwell lies north-west of Brandon. The sign stands in the garden of the Oak Street Almshouses and is not easy to find. Alveva, a Saxon woman who once owned part of the village, stands in the centre of the sign and behind are two large trees, an oak with a girth of 32 feet 6 inches (9.9 m), said to have been thirteen hundred years old when felled in 1964, and an elm felled two years before. The sheep represent ancient sheep walks and the church is shown as it was before the tower fell while under repair in 1898.

Downham Market is notable for its many Norfolk carr-stone buildings. Its sign, which was erected in 1965 to mark the fiftieth anniversary of the founding of the Downham Market Women's Institute, is two-sided. On one side St Winnold is seen ringing a bell, which, according to legend, caused fish to rise, and on the other young Nelson is playing with a toy ship — a reminder of Nelson's attendance at the local grammar school. One of the two small spandrels on either side of these panels bears the WI emblem and the other a butter churn, butter making having once been a local industry. The two white horses surmounting this handsome sign are a reminder of the horse fairs once held in the town, and they support a shield bearing the arms of Edmund, the martyr king, to whom the church is dedicated. The sign is situated in the town on the London road.

Brandon, on the Norfolk-Suffolk border, has long been noted for flint knapping, a trade which is still carried on there. In olden times the flints were brought from the nearby mines known as Grimes Graves. The sign, standing near the road junction at the southern end of the town, shows flint knappers at work.

Wretham. The group of villages known as the Wrethams is situated around the A1025 road from Thetford. Surrounded by the forested countryside of Breckland, it is an area of wild beauty, and the fine sign of coloured aluminium, which is to be found on the main road at the entrance to the village, depicts this; the witch and her cat flying across on her broomstick symbolise the belief in witchcraft in these remote areas. The ram's head surmounting it recalls an annual custom of the past, when the authorities of Eton College, which owned East Wretham, released a ram in a field, to be taken by whomever could catch it.

11

Hockham Magna, north-east of Thetford, was known in the past for the annual Hockham Horn Fair, at which objects of all kinds made of horn were sold. This was also the occasion for the appearance of the Horned Man who, in a horned head-dress, 'attacked' and chased strangers until they gave him money. The carved and painted sign, which stands on the village green, records this occasion in medieval times.

Thompson, a remote village a few miles south of Watton, stands beside the Peddars Way, an ancient track which ran from Holme on the Norfolk coast of the Wash, and its carved oak sign, which stands on the green at the crossroads, has figures of some who would have travelled that way. The coat of arms below is that of the Shardelow family, who founded a small college here in the fourteenth century.

Caston, a few miles south of Watton, had in medieval times a refectory which was visited by pilgrims on their way to the shrine at Walsingham. This later became Church Farm, and the gable end forms the background to the scene of pilgrims on the sign, which stands on the green before the church and in sight of Church Farm.

Watton has a gold-painted sign standing in the long High Street. Its theme is the story of the Babes in the Wood. It is reputed that the wood in the story is the nearby Wayland Wood, and that the wicked uncle lived in the neighbouring Griston Hall. The hare jumping over the tun represents the name Watton, 'wat' being a country word for a hare.

Saham Toney a village just north of Watton, has a fine church, by which the village sign stands, and nearby is a mere which is said to have appeared in a night. The mere, backed by numerous trees, is shown on the sign, and the boat with two clerical fishermen recalls that the monks from Castle Acre Priory were allowed to fish in the mere twice a year. The figure in the foreground, with his dog, is Sir Roger Toni, an early lord of the manor.

Brisley lies on the road from East Dereham to Fakenham, and the carved and coloured sign is by this road beside the church. Against a background of the church is the figure of Richard Taverner, who was born in the village and died in 1573. A scholar of both Oxford and Cambridge, he wrote and published an English translation of the Bible.

East Dereham. This busy town has an unusual sign which bridges the High Street. It was given by the Rotary Club in 1954 to mark the town's existence since 654. St Withburg, one of the saintly daughters of the Saxon king Anna, was first buried in East Dereham, though later her remains were removed by the monks to Ely. The sign, illustrating a legend, shows two does being pursued by a huntsman and seeking protection from the saint.

13

Ashill, south-east of Swaffham, has an attractive sign beside the large village green. The geese on the sign recall that, under the Enclosure Acts of the eighteenth century, each family in the village was allowed to graze not more than four geese on the green.

Stibbard, a village a few miles east of Fakenham, possesses a unique and arresting sign. It is the work of an internationally renowned sculptress, Ros Newman, and represents the agricultural life of the village for it depicts a ploughman at work. He and his plough are made from all manner of farm implements and bits and pieces of metal. The sign, which stands near the school, warrants time to study, for it is a fascinating work of art.

Gunthorpe, a rural village possessing a number of flint houses, lies between Fakenham and Holt. The sign, which stands on a grass triangle in the village at the junction of several roads, depicts two village benefactors who left legacies for the poor in what is known as the Malthouse Pightle Charity, the money being obtained from the rent of a small field or 'pightle'.

14

Fakenham has a two-sided sign which because of its siting is not seen to the best advantage. It stands at Leaches Corner, opposite the post office. The man at a printing press on the panel on one side represents the town's main industry. On the panel on the other side is the figure of Samuel Peckover, a Quaker and Cromwellian who opened Fakenham's first bank. The symbols on the brackets commemorate four other famous Fakenham men.

Thursford lies on the Fakenham to Holt road and its sign stands on a triangle of grass at Thursford Green. Nearby is the Thursford Collection of steam engines and mechanical organs and reference to this appears on the sign, along with many other items, which are described on a panel below the sign.

Great Walsingham won an award as the best kept village in 1972 and to commemorate this the inhabitants erected the sign, which stands on a small green in the centre of the village. The squirrel partly encircled by oak leaves is the crest of the Lee Warner family, long connected with the village.

Wells-next-the-Sea is a small town on the north Norfolk coast and its sign stands on the main road at the Holkham end. It was given by the Regatta and Carnival Committee and is in the shape of a square-rigged sail. The three-masted sailing ship in the centre, the lifeboat and the fish in the lower corners and the three cockle shells and oars below symbolise the town's connection with the sea, and the corn sheaf and plough in the upper corners its lesser link with agriculture.

Blakeney, a beautiful village and small harbour on the north Norfolk coast, possesses a fine sign which stands at one end of the quay. The ship in the centre records the three ships that were provided to Queen Elizabeth I to fight against the Spanish Armada. The fiddler and the cave-like hole on either side recall the story that a blind fiddler took a bet that he would fiddle his way down an underground passage, but he was never seen again. The waterfowl in the upper corners refer to the bird sanctuary at Blakeney Point. The hammers on the top of the sign are beetles used in clothmaking.

Langham is a small village a few miles inland from Blakeney. The sign, which stands opposite the Blue Bell, is a replacement of the original. On it, the ship commemorates the fact that Captain Marryat, the writer, once lived in the village and the turkey represents the turkey farm established on a wartime airfield nearby. Langham Hall was once the summer residence of the Bishop of Norwich — which accounts for the mitre surmounting the sign.

Holt. The sign, standing in front of Barclay's Bank, is two-sided. On one side is the figure of Sir John Gresham, former Lord Mayor of London, who in 1554 founded the free grammar school which later became Gresham's School. On the other side, in contrast, is Alice Perera, a notorious character of the fourteenth century. The owl on the top records that once a captured owl was put into the market pound. Even today the people of Holt are sometimes known as Holt Owls — this being also the name of the local football club.

Trunch. A little north of North Walsham is the village of Trunch. The church appears in the centre of the painted ironwork sign; at one side is the local brewery, built in 1837 but now closed, and at the other are a tractor and plough. The two smaller objects below are the village pump and the magnificent medieval font cover in the church. The sign is at the village crossroads, almost opposite the church.

Bodham, on the road from Holt to Cromer, gets its name, according to the Domesday Book, from a tax-collector named Boda who lived in the village. The sign, at the road junction in the village, shows him as a benevolent old man, apparently collecting taxes in kind.

Overstrand, on the coast just east of Cromer, possesses a two-sided sign on the Mundesley to Cromer road, at the corner of the High Street and the road to the beach, which records much of the village's past. The side shown in the photograph depicts a shipwreck, with one survivor who is being met by a local woman innkeeper, Rebecca Hythe, who was well known to sailors and smugglers. On the other side can be found the figures of a Dane and a Saxon, recording the struggles between these two peoples in the past, and a black dog, a fearsome legendary creature known as Black Shuck, who was said to bring misfortune if sighted. A crab and a poppy also appear on this interesting sign, the local crabs being amongst the finest and the poppy recalling the name Poppyland given to the area because of the countless poppies which grew there.

Swafield, a small village a little north of North Walsham, possesses an unusual and arresting sign. Made of metal and standing out against the sky is a wherry, such as used to carry coal from Great Yarmouth to Swafield Staithe. The massive post supporting the sign was the pivot of the post mill which once stood in the village. The sign is at the entrance to the village from North Walsham.

Paston, a small village a few miles south-east of Cromer on the coast road, is noteworthy as the home of the Paston family, writers of the famous Paston letters of the fifteenth century. Its most striking feature is the large Paston Barn, an Elizabethan building of flint and thatch. There is also a restored windmill. The unusual swinging sign, at the side of the road by the post office, records all these features.

Happisburgh, pronounced Haisborough, a village on the north-east coast of Norfolk south-east of Cromer, has strong connections with the sea, including a prominent lighthouse. Its church has a tower 110 feet (34 m) high, which has long served as a landmark for sailors, and in the churchyard lie more than a hundred sailors shipwrecked on the dangerous Happisburgh sands. The church also contains a beautiful octagonal font, at which it is recorded that on Whit Sunday 1793 the parson baptised 120 children. The sign, which stands by the road below the church, depicts the baptism at the font, the church and the lighthouse, together with a lifeboat and, representing the agricultural activity of the village, some corn. The figures on either side are Edric, a Danish overlord of the eleventh century, and Maud, a daughter of Roger Bigod, who received the manor from the king in about 1100 and was thought to have been buried here.

Worstead. The cloth called worsted, which is now produced in Yorkshire, was originally made in Worstead, south of North Walsham. Now just a charming village, in which a number of the old weavers' houses are still to be found, it was in the past a fair-sized town, with two churches; and its present church is one of the great ones of Norfolk. The sign, standing just outside the west end of the church, shows the church, with a horned sheep and the coat of arms of the Worstead family.

Felthorpe, a few miles north-west of Norwich, has an unusually shaped sign. It is a circular drum, on which is a painting of Felthorpe Hall, a fine residence noted for its numerous daffodils. The sign, which stands near the village hall, is made entirely of metal — appropriately, as the manufacture of agricultural implements was once a local industry.

Hevingham, between Norwich and Aylsham, is a village which was noted for its broom making. The village sign, which stands on the green in the part of the village known as Westgate, recalls this with its crossed brooms against a background which includes the church. The sign was the idea of one of the last of the brushmakers in the village.

South Walsham is near the broad named after it and not far from Acle. On the green stands the sign, which was given by the local Women's Institute. In Saxon times the people were in constant fear of invasion by the Vikings, and the sign shows a Viking ship sailing up the river, watched by a Saxon warrior. Behind are the two village churches, one now in ruins, and a wind pump.

Sprowston. The sign, wrought in metal and painted bright red, is outstanding. It is the work of Sprowston Secondary School and stands at the side of the road from Norwich to Wroxham. The post mill depicted on it appears in a number of pictures by John Crome, one of which is in the National Gallery. The mill was burnt down in 1933. A falcon is shown hovering above the fifteenth-century parish church, falconry having been practised here in the past.

Thorpe End is a pleasant garden suburb a few miles east of Norwich. The sign, which stands on a green by the side of the Norwich to Acle road, has the sky as its background. The central carving in wood of an oak tree in a triangular frame formed the original sign, the work of an architect who designed a number of the local houses. It was later enclosed in the wrought iron frame with the figures of a man and a woman gardening.

Salhouse is one of several attractive villages lying a few miles north-west of Norwich, in an area in which reeds are cut for Norfolk reed thatching, the best and longest lasting type of thatch. The name Salhouse is derived from sallow, a dwarf species of willow, out of which pegs are made for thatching. The sign, which is carved and brightly painted, stands on a triangle of grass before the Bell Inn. On it are shown two men cutting reeds, with a boat sailing on the nearby broad, and, above, an arch of sallows supporting the name of the village.

Potter Heigham has two village signs. One is in the old village and the other, illustrated here, is by the medieval bridge about a mile away. On one side are two Roman potters; pottery was produced in the old village in Roman times. On the other, the scene of sailing boats, a fisherman and a birdwatcher refers to present-day pastimes; and below is a man digging peat. Surmounting this colourful sign is the arched bridge.

Somerleyton is recorded in the Domesday Book as *Sumeledetun,* meaning a summer expedition or band of plundering Danes. The sign, which stands in the centre of the village, portrays a Viking and his ship and was erected in the village by Lord and Lady Somerleyton on the occasion of their silver wedding anniversary in 1949.

Beccles was once a flourishing port but now caters mainly for Broadland cruisers and yachts. Its handsome houses are mostly Georgian, as most of the Tudor buildings were destroyed by fires; but the sign tells of these earlier times for it shows Queen Elizabeth I presenting the municipal charter to the Port Reeve. It stands in a commanding position on the Bungay road.

Loddon is a delightful town of beautiful eighteenth-and early nineteenth-century buildings, and the houses built by the local council blend perfectly with these. The sign is a striking figure, cast in bronze, of Alfric, called Modercope, the original Saxon lord of Loddon, who gave the lordship to Bury St Edmunds Abbey in the reign of Edward the Confessor. His hand rests on a replica of the poor box, cut out of solid oak, which is in the church and said to be one of the oldest in England. The sign is at the crossroads, almost opposite the church.

Martham lies between the coast at Winterton and the Norfolk Broadland, and so the sign, which stands on the green, shows on one side a Saxon woman pleading for mercy from a Viking invader and on the other a Norfolk wherry, typical of those which traded on the rivers, and a windmill pump, such as was used to drain the marshes.

Caister-on-Sea, on the coast north of Yarmouth, was an important town in Roman times. Today it is notable for its fishing community and for its lifeboat, which has saved many lives on this dangerous coast. The carved wooden sign, which stands in the town in front of the police station, depicts on one side the head of a Roman soldier and on the other a lifeboat of early design battling against the seas.

Geldeston, a village north-west of Beccles, lies amidst beautiful countryside on the Norfolk-Suffolk border. Its carved and painted sign stands on the green and illustrates various features of the countryside and the many activities which used to be or still are carried on around. In the centre is a wherry, such as used to carry corn, seen sailing up the river to the old maltings.

Framingham Earl is south-east of Norwich near the Bungay road, and its sign, which is by the side of this road, stands out sharply as it is made of pierced and wrought iron and painted. The figure in the centre is the Earl of Norfolk — the Earl in the village name — and he is surrounded by tall trees, recording the trees planted in and around the village during the nineteenth century by an eminent Norwich surgeon, Edward Rigby, whose tombstone is in the churchyard of the Saxon-Norman church.

Earsham, just west of Bungay, is well known as the headquarters of the Otter Trust, whose lands include three lakes and a small stream, as well as breeding enclosures for the otters; it is a beautiful and peaceful place to visit. The sign, which is opposite the road to the hall, shows an otter surmounting a scene which includes the watermill, no longer in use, as it was in 1793.

Bungay is a town which has been an important crossing place of the river Waveney at least since Roman times, and its present castle was built by Roger Bigod in 1294 on the site of an even earlier one. The castle appears arrestingly on the sign, which stands at the entrance to the town on the Ipswich road.

Trowse Newton lies a few miles south-east of Norwich on the Beccles road, and the sign stands on the main road by the bridge. It illustrates the legend that a villager, disgruntled with his neighbours, built himself a house in a tree. The name Trowse is derived from the Old English *tre-hus*, tree house.

Saxlingham Nethergate, a village several miles south of Norwich, possesses many trees and a beautiful Elizabethan hall. On the green, before the church and the hall, stands the carved oak sign, which shows the figure of a Saxon who founded the village in AD 832.

Wymondham is a town with fine old buildings and an equally fine abbey, and its two-sided sign, which is at the corner of Church Street in front of the county library, tells of its past. On one side Robert Kett, a Wymondham man who became the leader of the rebellion against the enclosure of common lands, is seen encouraging others to join with him. On the other is a wood-turner, for Wymondham was noted for this work and the arms of the town, which appear below, bear a wooden spoon crossed by a spigot. Over all is a carved model of the abbey, before which stands a Benedictine monk.

22

Hempnall is a village on the B1135 road from Bungay to Wymondham. John Wesley came here to preach in 1754 and recorded in his journal: 'The ring leader of the mob came with his horn, as usual, before I began, but one quickly catched and threw away his horn, and in a few minutes he was deserted by all his companions who were seriously attentive to the great truth. By grace ye are saved through faith.' The occasion is shown on the village sign, which is a fine example of work produced by combined local effort and talent. It stands at the road junction near the church.

Hingham is a large village a few miles east of Watton. It was here that Samuel Lincoln, an ancestor of Abraham, worked as a weaver, before going to Norwich and finally to America in the steps of the Pilgrim Fathers. They and their ships are represented on the sign, which stands on the green by the post office.

Hethersett, a few miles from Wymondham on the way to Norwich, is skirted by the A11 road, and the sign stands just off this road at the Norwich end of the village. It is finely carved in natural wood and shows the fourteenth-century church, a deer, referring to the village's old name of *Hederseta,* meaning an enclosure for deer, and a formal-style oak tree representing the tree still standing by the side of the A11, under which Robert Kett is said to have raised his rebellion in 1549.

Fritton, east of Long Stratton, possesses a large common. This can be pleasantly viewed from the village sign, which is situated on a corner of the common and has a hexagonal base which provides seats all round. The figure of the ploughman shows that this is an agricultural area and the squirrel and the owl on the brackets typify the wildlife.

East Harling, some miles north-east of Thetford, has a finely carved sign with various motifs on the post and, above, an enchanting lamb symbolising the Lamb Fair which was held annually in July. Standing on the village green, it was presented by the Boy Scouts on the occasion of the coronation of Queen Elizabeth II in 1953.

Quidenham is a small village surrounded by woodland, lying off the Thetford to Norwich road. It is believed to be the burial place of Boadicea, or Boudica, the queen of the Iceni and she appears on the sign driving her chariot. The sign, of wrought iron and painted, is to be found on the village green, where it stands out clearly against the sky.

Bressingham, a village to the west of Diss, is known for its park-like plant nursery and collection of steam engines. These are on the road from Diss to Thetford, but the village and the church are a little to the north of it, and the sign, erected to commemorate the golden jubilee in 1973 of the local Women's Institute, is in the village at Pillar Box Corner. The original church was built in 1280 by Sir Richard Boyland, a judge who was fined 4000 marks by King Edward II for corruption. The sign portrays him, standing in front of the church.

Thetford, on the Norfolk-Suffolk border, is a town which is a mixture of old flint and timber-framed houses and new industrial buildings. The sign, which stands on the right of the A11 road from London, is two-sided. On one side stands Sweyne, king of the Danes, who made Thetford his capital and died there, and on the other Thomas Paine, author of *The Rights of Man* and supporter of the American Revolution, who was born there in 1737.

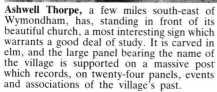

Ashwell Thorpe, a few miles south-east of Wymondham, has, standing in front of its beautiful church, a most interesting sign which warrants a good deal of study. It is carved in elm, and the large panel bearing the name of the village is supported on a massive post which records, on twenty-four panels, events and associations of the village's past.

Diss, on the river Waveney just inside the Nokfolk border, is a bustling modern town but has many old houses dating back to Tudor times. It is built round a 6 acre (2.4 ha) mere or lake, beside which stands the two-sided sign. John Skelton, rector of Diss from 1504 to 1529 and Poet Laureate, was tutor to the children of Henry VII and is shown, on one side of the sign, with the royal children. On the other side are two figures of an earlier period, explained on a plate below.

Southwold is a delightful town on the Suffolk coast which has a number of Georgian houses and a small musueum. The sign, which is across the road from the post office, depicts two men of war, one flying the British flag, the other the Dutch, commemorating the terrible and indecisive Battle of Sole Bay fought, in full view of the townsfolk, between the English and the Dutch fleets in 1672.

Kenninghall, lies in the centre of the triangle formed by Thetford, Diss and Attleborough. On the green at the crossroads is the brightly coloured wrought iron sign. The coats of arms on the four shields are those of Edward the Confessor (top), the Howards, Dukes of Norfolk (left), the Earl of Mowbray (right) and the Earl of Albemarle (below). The riderless horse and the hound, the badge of the Talbots, both represent carvings in the village church. At the top of the sign is the Kenninghall Brooch, an Anglo-Saxon ornament found near where the sign stands.

Scole, which lies just in Norfolk on the border with Suffolk, has been a staging post of importance since Roman times, the name meaning a shelter. The sign stands on a green by the war memorial, not far from the White Hart, a posting inn built in 1655. On the sign is the head of a Roman eagle and crossed posthorns. Below are the shields of two families who were lords of the manor and the Saltire of St Andrew, to whom the nearby church is dedicated.

Pulham St Mary, north-east of Scole, has an unusual motif for its sign, which stands in the centre of the village. The airship tethered to its mooring mast is the R33, sometimes known as the Pulham Pig, which was built in a hangar near the former Pulham railway station.

Fressingfield, a village midway between Scole and Halesworth, is noted for its inn, the Fox and Goose, and for one of the finest small churches in Suffolk. It was the site of a pilgrims' hospice, being on the route to the shrine at Walsingham from the port of Dunwich. This is recalled in the sign in the village showing a pilgrim with his mule.

26

Walberswick, a village of great charm on the Suffolk coast across the River Blyth from Southwold, was once a much bigger place. There are many large old houses, and ships were built and manned there. Its painted copper sign of a sailing ship (above left) stands commandingly on the grassy bank beside the road at the entrance to the village.

Westleton is a fine village a few miles inland from Dunwich on the Suffolk coast. The sign, which is of wrought iron painted black and white, depicts the old windmill which stood in the village until its demolition in 1963. A sail beam of the old mill forms the post for the sign and at the base is a millstone. The sign stands prominently at the top of the village green.

Middleton, down a turning off the A12 road at Yoxford, is a delightful and almost hidden Suffolk village. Its two-sided sign, showing on one side a colourful cock and on the other the church, before which it stands, is unique, being made of mosaic, the work of a local artist.

Kelsale cum Carlton has, standing on the A12 Ipswich to Yarmouth road, a wrought iron sign of the kind frequently found in villages in this area. Kelsale is noted for its vineyard and in the centre of the sign hangs a bunch of grapes and circling this are the eight bells of the church.

Sibton. Near Yoxford on the Yoxford to Stowmarket road is the village of Sibton, and on a high bank opposite the church is the village sign, standing out sharply against the sky. The monks in white habits and the sheep record that the Cistercian monastery in Sibton was the only one in Suffolk where the monks were sheep farmers.

Peasenhall is a few miles along the road from Sibton towards Stowmarket, and the sign is by this road in the centre of the village. Of wrought iron and painted, it is a model of a Smyth seed-drill, such as was made in the Peasenhall works of Smyth and Son from 1800 to 1967.

Haughley, a few miles north of Stowmarket, has, standing in the centre of the village, a wrought iron sign representing a motte and bailey castle, the remains of which are to be found at the northern end of the village.

Brandeston is a small village away from the main roads a few miles south-west of Framlingham. Its wrought iron sign is on a triangle of grass opposite the Queen's Head. On it, the hanging figure beside the fourteenth-century church is that of one of its past vicars, John Lowes, who was hanged for witchcraft in 1646; and the cottage is that reputedly used as a hideaway by the famous smuggler Margaret Catchpole, who was finally deported to New South Wales. The arms above are those of the Revetts, an old Brandeston family and benefactors of the church.

Woolpit, a most attractive village east of Bury St Edmunds, gets its name from having had pits for trapping wolves. Its beautiful church has a Victorian spire which can be seen for miles around. It also has a legend of two Green Children, a boy and a girl, who, in the reign of King Stephen, came out of the ground into a harvest field and were cared for in the village, gradually losing their green colour when their diet was changed from bean pith to bread; the girl eventually married a man from King's Lynn, but the boy died soon after baptism. A wolf, the church spire and the children appear on the wrought iron sign which stands beside the church — the children appropriately painted green.

Drinkstone is a few miles east of Bury St Edmunds, and its sign is to be found at Drinkstone Green, at the entrance to a close of new houses. Designed and carved by a local resident from an oak cut from a nearby estate, it depicts a mill which still stands outside Drinkstone and it is protected by a roof of wooden shingles.

Earl Soham lies midway between Stowmarket and Yoxford, and standing on the green, surrounded by fine trees, is a most striking sign. In medieval times Earl Soham was a centre for falconry, and the tall carved figure of a falconer with his bird recalls this sport. The Women's Institute commissioned the Ipswich School of Art to do the work and the sign was erected in 1953 to commemorate the Queen's coronation. It was restored in 1979.

West Stow, north of Bury St Edmunds, is the site of an Anglo-Saxon settlement, which the St Edmundsbury Borough Council has made into a country park, with pleasant woodland and walks, around a reconstruction of the settlement. Two of these Anglo-Saxon houses appear on the sign, which stands in the village at the junction of the Bury St Edmunds and Mildenhall roads and was painted by the art master of the nearby Culford School and erected in 1977 by the Women's Institute.

Stonham Parva is close to the A140 road from Ipswich to Norwich. Its painted wrought iron sign recalls that this road has long been an important highway, along which many coaches used to travel. The magpie represents the coaching inn of that name which still stands in the village. The sign, which is not easily found, is in the village on the main road.

Great Finborough, a pleasant village just south-west of Stowmarket, has a fine wrought iron sign standing on the green, not far from the tall-spired church. It is well sited and stands out clearly against the sky. The tall oak in the centre represents one of many planted by the squire, and the man and woman and sheaf of corn symbolise life and fertility. The border of chestnut leaves refers to the numerous chestnut trees in the locality.

Pakenham, north-east of Bury St Edmunds, has both a windmill and a watermill. They both appear, under a carving of the church, on the sign, which stands in the village beside the village hall.

Easton, a few miles north-west of Wickham Market, well warrants a visit for it is a charming setting of houses, large and small, surrounded by fine trees. It is also the home of the Easton Harriers, and this is the subject of the village sign, which stands on grass beside the road below the church. The background to the placename represents the crinkle-crankle wall of the Easton Park estate.

Orford, although an important port in Elizabethan times, is now only a large village. Its imposing castle was built by Henry II in 1165. The keep, which is all that remains, was the first in England to be built in hexagonal shape. Its dungeon, according to a fifteenth-century story, once held a Wild Man, half man and half fish, who was caught in a fisherman's net but later escaped back into the sea. The sign, which stands at the entrance to the village, by the school, depicts the castle.

Benhall. The wrought iron sign stands at the entrance to the village on the A12 Ipswich to Yarmouth road, just south of Saxmundham. The Suffolk plough, supported by half wheels, is painted blue. The sign was put up in memory of the village postmaster, Ted Ayden.

FURTHER READING

Proctor, Frances, and Miller, Philippa. *Village Signs in Norfolk.*
Proctor, Frances, and Miller, Philippa. *100 More Village Signs of the County of Norfolk.*
Proctor, Frances, and Miller, Philippa. *Book 3, Village Signs of Norfolk.*

INDEX

ACKNOWLEDGEMENTS

I gratefully acknowledge the help I have received from several people: Mrs Molly Carter, whose appreciation of and enthusiasm for her late husband's work, and the help she gave me, greatly contributed to this book; Philippa Miller and Frances Proctor, who allowed me to use their photographs of the signs of the villages on the Sandringham estate; Mr E. F. Hardy of Stowmarket, whose well illustrated talk on village signs initially inspired me to write this book and who gave me help later; and last, but by no means least, my husband, who has given me great encouragement and assistance.

INTRODUCTION

Wheels around Lanarkshire is the eighteenth Scottish book in this nostalgic transport series. Lanarkshire is a large county with a great diversity of territory and transport interest from the more industrial north to the attractive countryside of the south. One of my own abiding memories of Lanarkshire is that it was a county of red buses (mainly Central SMT) and red roads, some of which remain in rural areas. Council lorries would load up with red granite chips from Cairngryffe Quarry, near Carmichael, to spread on their highways and byways, which to my mind enhanced them by projecting a friendlier and more individual appearance than roads in other counties. This book is simply a taster which can only include a fraction of the material available, some of which will be included in future "Wheels" books on specific areas of the county. I hope you enjoy this overview of some fondly remembered examples of bygone transport from tramcars to trains in a variety of Lanarkshire locations from collieries to the countryside.

Robert Grieves.

Little is known about this friendly photograph other than it was taken somewhere in Lanarkshire in the early 1920s showing a Royal Enfield motor cycle of the period registered in the county as V 6963. Crash helmets werre not obligatory at that time, but perhaps the headgear of the 1920s was a good substitute. The Royal Enfield name first appeared in 1893 but the firm ceased business in the UK in 1970. However, the famous marque is now built in Chennai (Madras) India and is considered to be the oldest motor cycle company in the world still in production.

This happy scene, which appears to be perhaps a huge Sunday School outing, dates from 1909. All the vehicles were owned by a Wishaw firm grandly known as the British Motor Express Company. The leading charabanc was V 773, a Belhaven built in Wishaw by Robert Morton and Sons and also bodied in the town by John Steel and Co., followed by two of what were surely amongst the earliest double deck buses in Scotland. Both were built on ABC chassis, the foremost registered V 786. The All British Car Co. of Bridgeton (ABC) was founded in 1905 by George Johnston, who left his Arrol-Johnston Car Co. of Paisley to establish the firm. An over-ambitious annual production target of 750 cars and commercials never came to fruition. Only a handful of vehicles were built including these two double deckers. Some of the ABC commercials featured Arrol-Johnston engines. The rearmost charabanc in the line is a Mutel wagonette imported from Paris.

V 574 was a 20 h.p. Halley owned in 1908 by John Gibson of Wishaw for a passenger service between Wishaw and Newmains. Later that year Gibson was one of a partnership who started the "West Lothian Motor Service" in Bathgate, operating Halleys to Armadale, Seafield and Uphall. The conductor, in short trousers, is on the front step while his passengers are all open to the elements in the very basic solid tyred wagonette and immune to any discomfort as nothing better was available. No superior transport option existed in the area at that time, since Lanarkshire Tramways did not extend their system from Wishaw to Newmains until 1909.

Belhaven commercial chassis were built from about 1906 by Robert Morton & Son Ltd., Heathery Road, Wishaw. Steam powered vehicles were produced initially, followed by petrol driven lorries and buses first using Tyler then Aster engines. For his first two buses pioneer operator Walter Alexander of Falkirk chose Belhaven. The Scottish Co-operative Wholesale Society bought Belhaven lorries in quantity, but badged them under their own trade name "Unitas". The scene above, from around 1910, shows Belhaven lorries in service with Archibald's toffee mills of Wishaw, the one on the right being V 991 (claimed to be the first confectionery motor lorry in Scotland) and driven by James Stewart, who later started his own bus and lorry hiring business in Wishaw, latterly specialising in removals. A railway siding, visible in the photo, ran into the "Battleaxe" factory, believed to have been Scotland's largest confectionery works in Edwardian days.

In addition to Belhaven, Wishaw was home to Mackay and Jardine, who built Clyde commercial vehicles in the town from around 1913 and also buses after the 1914-18 hostilities. Joseph Mackay had formerly been works manager with Belhaven and George Jardine had also been an employee. They are both seen here (Mackay standing) in Glen Road, Wishaw, at the entrance to the Belhaven estate with V 3734, one of the earliest examples of a Clyde chain-driven 3-tonner, supplied to the town's Strathclyde Bakery. This 1913 model was fitted with an Aster petrol engine, but after 1918 Clydes were assembled using a combination of Buda engines (imported from the USA), Fuller gearboxes and Sheldon back axles, with chassis frames built by Mechans of Scotstoun. Increasing competition from mass-produced rivals such as Chevrolet caused the demise of Clyde production and in 1933 Mackay and Jardine started a Bedford agency in Wishaw, finally selling out to Parks of Hamilton in the 1970s.

A later Clyde lorry is this example which was supplied to flour millers and grain merchant James MacGregor of Garrion Mills in 1925. Note that solid tyres were still a feature at this date. MacGregor also had a base at the Town Mill, Strathaven and used a livery of light grey with red lining and red mudguards for his transport fleet. Later lorries included Morris Commercials and six wheel Albions. The company motto painted on the front of their lorries and against the background of a hessian sack was *"For man, beast or fowl, better canna be"*. The official illustration by local photographer Charles Reid was taken in Kenilworth Avenue, Wishaw, not far from the premises of coachbuilder John Stewart in Kirk Road who constructed the bodywork on this vehicle.

John Plenderleith of Symington at the wheel of the foremost member of this motoring trio of hire cars outside his garage in Biggar Road, Symington shortly after World War I. The cars, all registered in Lanarkshire, are V 4316 (a Humber 14 of 1913 vintage), V 6393 (an Overland) and V 5782, one of the ubiquitous model T Fords, which ensured immortality for Henry, this one notably with left hand drive. Production of the model T lasted from 1908 until 1927 with an incredible 16.5 million examples built, making it the world's most popular car until overtaken in the 1970s by the Volkswagen "Beetle".

The forecourt of Plenderleith's Tinto Garage in Symington with two of their hire cars in 1928. Mechanics explore the innards of VA 6386, a 12 h.p. Fiat saloon of 1927, while VA 5615, a 1926 Armstrong Siddeley 14 h.p. saloon, is refuelled with petrol from the Shell Mex pump by employee George Urquhart in gaiters and white topped cap. He served in the dual role of mechanic and chauffeur, which also involved driving Plenderleith's Tinto buses on the route between Lanark and Biggar when the fleet included an assortment of Dennis, Unic, Lancia and Albion vehicles. John Plenderleith himself supervises proceedings from the left of this scene and in 1929 he sold the business to Taggarts of Knowetop, Motherwell. Today the Tinto Garage is owned by James Harvie.

Henry Archibald who owned the Battleaxe toffee factory in Wishaw or toffee mills as he named it, was also an enthusiastic motorist. Around the time when he operated the Belhaven lorries seen on page 5 he was also owner of this fine Alexandria-built Argyll open tourer. Unfortunately, during an outing on a sunny summer day in 1912 the Argyll suffered a rear offside puncture and Henry is seen changing the wheel while his wife and two sons John and Henry Junior wait patiently in the car. This side view clearly shows the Argyll's gate type gear change system outside the coachwork, featuring two gear levers and also the long snake-like bulb horn adjacent to the driver's right hand; the long handbrake lever is also visible. In those far off days it was only a small group of the more affluent citizens in any community who could afford the very high purchase price of an automobile, the cost of which was then proportionately much higher than now.

Archibald Scott of Bellshill was one of several prominent coach builders in Lanarkshire, now no longer in business. Founded in 1877 the firm originally supplied horse drawn broughams, cabs, carts and vans to butchers, bakers and the like in the surrounding area. On the arrival of the motor age Scotts adapted to embrace the new forms of transport and built up a much wider customer base as the quality of their product was appreciated further afield. More recently they specialised in minibuses, travelling shops and ice cream vans particularly on Ford Transit and Bedford chassis, supplied to clients throughout the country and overseas as far afield as the Middle East, Nigeria and the West Indies. The upper illustration shows V 3082 a chain-driven, solid-tyred lorry with chassis built by Belhaven of Wishaw in 1913 prior to delivery to wholesale merchants Cassels & Co. of Hamilton.

The lower view depicts VA 5358, a Dodge bus supplied in 1926 to Samuel Colville of Mossend, Bellshill, one of several operators on the busy route between Glasgow, Tannochside, Bellshill and Newarthill. He called his vehicle *Lady of the Lake* in the period when naming individual members of the fleet was popular with many companies. Both pictures were taken at Scott's Coachworks in North Road, Bellshill.

James Hunter & Sons operated from premises in Kitchener Street, Wishaw both as haulage contractors and charabanc proprietors. Starting in business in Edwardian times the firm's haulage side originated with horses and carts on general deliveries around the Wishaw area. Hunter's foresight allowed an early entry into the era of motor transport and prior to World War I the first such vehicles joined the fleet. These included Belhavens, Karriers and Leylands, all of which could be used as delivery lorries during the week and then converted to charabancs at the weekend to capture the private hire and excursion trade. The lorry illustrated was a Karrier K4 type four-tonner pictured at the Karrier works in Huddersfield prior to delivery in 1921 and before licensing. The Karrier charabanc was one of the first vehicles to be registered with the local GM letters covering Motherwell & Wishaw. This was GM 18 of 1920 and the typical charabanc body with a separate door to each row of seats could be removed and the conversion made to a lorry when required.

Opposite: V 4762 is a further example of a Karrier commercial chassis working as a lorry but which could also be adapted to carry a charabanc body (similar to that shown left). This one was originally in the fleet of haulage contractor James Hunter of Wishaw in 1919, but is seen here after its sale to Whiteford of East Nemphlar. James Whiteford is at the wheel in Wellgatehead, Lanark on one of many journeys he made with pipes for Sir William Arrol's construction work at the Falls of Clyde hydro-electric power scheme in 1926. The pipes were delivered by rail to Lanark Station, then somewhat precariously by lorry to the work site in a manner which would be frowned on by today's health and safety officers. On top of the pipe is a jack giving tension to the rope securing the load. Another interesting feature is the Karrier's radiator filler cap which shows the popular Great War character "Ole Bill" created by artist Bruce Bairnsfather. Whitefords remained in business latterly as coach operators (Nationwide Coaches) until acquisition by Wilson of Carnwath in 1990.

13

John Carmichael of Airdrie served as a sergeant in the Prince of Wales Regiment during the Great War when he committed an act of extreme bravery for which he was awarded the supreme honour of the Victoria Cross. On his return he bought a poultry farm at Glenmavis, but around 1921 started the bus operations for which he became best known. John (left) is seen with brother Tom in this view of one of his earliest buses, taken at the Meadows in Glenmavis where they were kept. This was solid tyred Leyland V 6703 which like John Carmichael himself had served in the Great War. These former War Department vehicles were reconditioned by Leyland Motors and sold at attractive prices to many ex-servicemen who used their gratuities to start a small transport business. This charabanc was used on the passenger service Carmichael initiated between Coatbridge, Glenboig and Kilsyth, a route which he continued to operate under the fleet name Highland Bus Service until finally selling out to Walter Alexander & Sons (Midland) Ltd. in 1966. From 1933 Carmichael's buses were based at Greenfoot Garage, Glenboig and although the choice of Highland as the name for a firm based in Lanarkshire may seem strange it can be explained by the Carmichael family having come originally from the island of Lismore.

John Cuthill Sword was another native of Airdrie who became a well known entrepreneur in the world of transport, not only by road but also in the air. The son of a baker in Airdrie, he worked as a van man selling bread and cakes in the town before joining the Royal Flying Corps during the 1914-18 war. Smitten by both the motoring and aviation bugs he opened a garage in Loudon Street from where he dealt in motoring accessories and additionally operated as a haulage contractor between Airdrie and Glasgow. He also started bus services between Coatbridge and Gartcosh and from Coatbridge to Annathill and Kilsyth, at first using an ex W.D. Talbot ambulance converted to a charabanc with wooden seats and open sides. In 1925 he extended his operations by opening up his Midland service in competition with the Glasgow Corporation trams between Glasgow and Paisley (soon extending to Johnstone) and between Clarkston, Airdrie and Glasgow. Further services from Glasgow ran to Ardrossan, Ayr, Castle Douglas, Dumfries, Kilmarnock and Stranraer. Express buses ran to Blackpool and to London. In 1932 John Sword became general manager of the newly-formed Western SMT Co. and director of the various other companies forming the Scottish Motor Traction group. Sword's pioneering aviation operations were based at Renfrew aerodrome by his company Midland & Scottish Air Ferries Ltd. including Scotland's first airline service which flew to Campbeltown in April 1933. One of several other diverse businesses started by this remarkable man was Crimpy Crisps Ltd., of Cairnhill Road, Airdrie. In 1951 John Sword deservedly received the freedom of the Burgh of Airdrie in recognition of the benefits he had brought to his native town.

The illustration shows VA 3831, one of a large fleet of Albion buses in Sword's red liveried Midland fleet, seen here in 1925 with a group of employees outside the garage in Gartlea Road, Airdrie before a move was made to larger premises in Carlisle Road. This was a 24 h.p. model with 20 seat body by Northern Counties of Wigan. The boss in a bunnet, John Sword himself, stands at the extreme right.

VA 3005 was no.14 in the large Leyland fleet of J.D. Hendry & Sons, Coatbridge. This was a dual entrance SG9 model of 1924, with solid tyres which at a later date were converted to pneumatics. Hendry's busy main route served Glasgow, Coatbridge, Airdrie and Clarkston, where this view was taken with the crew and a friend. Conductress Jenny McWhirter has her right hand on her cash bag and rack of tickets, which when issued were clipped by means of the "Bell Punch" strapped over her shoulder. Hendry's fleet was acquired in 1926 by the expanding Scottish Motor Traction Company of Edinburgh, giving them a first foothold on the west side of the country. This bus, however, was not one of those which passed to SMT but was instead sold to Webster Bros., of Wigan and later became no. 353 in the giant fleet of Ribble Motor Services, Preston.

William Irvine of Glenmavis started the first bus service between the village and Airdrie in 1920, with a model T Ford, followed by a GMC with 14 seat bodywork converted from a wartime ambulance. Shown above is Irvine's first proper bus which was VA 5322, a 20 seat Buda engined Clyde bodied by Stewart of Wishaw and bought in 1926. By this time a service was also operated between Coatbridge and Gartcosh, the location of this view with driver John Lang and conductor MacDonald, proudly standing beside their new blue bus. Services were later developed between Greengairs, Rigghead, Rawyards and Airdrie and also from the old mining community of Darngavel to Airdrie via Whiterigg and Airdriehill, while the fleet livery was changed to maroon. An assortment of Albion, Clyde, Commer, Daimler, Dennis and Leyland buses represented Irvine's mixed fleet when the firm sold out in 1940 to SMT, but not before the poem of praise above was penned by driver Jimmy Kerr.

The maroon liveried buses of J. W. & R. Torrance of Hamilton were a familiar sight on the route between Hamilton, Blantyre and Glasgow in the second half of the 1920s. John Torrance had been an electrical engineer based in Campbell Street, Hamilton on the site where Stirlings pioneering coach works had been, but realising the potential of the motorbus inaugurated his first passenger service in 1924. A few Italian-built Lancia buses were used initially, but were soon superseded by the more reliable Albion from Scotstoun which featured strongly in the fleet until the business was sold in 1930 to the LMS railway company. The LMS retained the Torrance name until formation of the Central SMT Co. Ltd. in 1932 when the former Torrance buses received their new owner's dark red colours, which were to remain familiar throughout Lanarkshire into the 1980s. Many of the buses continued to be garaged at the Burnbank Road depot near Peacock Cross in Hamilton which had been purpose-built by Torrance and remained as a bus depot with Central SMT until 1962. This animated view from 1925 shows VA 3321, one of Torrance's original fleet of Lancia buses, seen straddling the tramlines in Kirk Road, Wishaw about to depart for Hamilton and Glasgow. The top deck of a Newmains-bound tram may just be seen disappearing over the horizon while one of Barr's horsedrawn wagons delivers lemonade and of course Iron Brew (as it was originally spelled). Barr's retained a depot in Wishaw until 2005 when all work was then centralised at their new premises in Cumbernauld .

An advert from 1928 for the Glasgow General Omnibus & Motor Services Ltd., usually known as GOC, featuring one of its AEC buses. This company entered the transport business in Lanarkshire in a big way in 1926 with plenty of financial capital which the existing small private companies lacked . It was later to form the main basis for the newly formed Central SMT company in 1932. Using a big fleet of AEC and later ADC vehicles painted in a striking red livery, routes were opened up to many parts of the county including Hamilton, Newton, Newmains, Netherburn, Shotts, Coalburn, Larkhall, Strathaven and Douglas. As the company expanded, many of its smaller rivals were unable to compete and accordingly either gave up business or sold out to the mushrooming GOC. Services were also operated from Glasgow along the north bank of the Clyde to Balloch and to Helensburgh in Dunbartonshire from the new covered premises purpose-built by GOC in Waterloo Street, which was the city's first bus station, opened in 1928. This continued to be used by Central SMT and Western SMT until closure in 1971 when Anderston Bus Station opened. This has also been closed, with Buchanan remaining as the sole city bus station.

Hamilton (Hammy) Jackson of Auchenheath started his bus business in the early 1920s, connecting the towns of Lanark and Lesmahagow via the villages of Kirkfieldbank, Auchenheath, Dillarburn and Braehead. Occasional journeys continued via Kirkmuirhill, Boghead and Sandford to Strathaven which in the 1950s and 1960s had a running time of 1hour 10 minutes, much quicker than the Central SMT timing of 1hour 50 minutes for its circuitous route between Lanark and Strathaven via Douglas, Glespin, Glenbuck, Linkyburn, Muirkirk and Dungavel. This scene shows Jackson's original garage at Auchenheath in the late 1920s, with Hammy standing to the left of his little 14 seat Clyde bus. This was SP 4589 and had been new in 1921 to Forrester of Lochgelly in Fife, passing later to Cleland of Bogside, Newmains from whom Jackson bought it. The car was a Morris Oxford *Bullnose* used for hiring.

Storming up Lanark High Street emitting a cloud of exhaust smoke which almost obscures the baby Austin car following and which would not be tolerated under today's strict standards, is one of Hamilton Jackson's blue double deckers bound for the town's horsemarket bus stance from where it will start its journey to Lesmahagow. This was a former Glasgow Corporation A.E.C. Regent of 1938 with bodywork by Weymann and appropriately registered BUS 165. Hammy purchased two of these in 1952 at a time when business was buoyant. However, as more people were able to purchase cars in an improving economy, patronage accordingly dropped on what was a largely rural service and in 1962 Jackson sold the run to Whiteford of Lanark who continued the operation until it passed to the current operator Stokes bus service of Carstairs.

The Lanarkshire Tramways Company, or the Hamilton, Motherwell and Wishaw Tramways Company as it was originally named, commenced operations in July 1903 between Blantyre and Wishaw. In 1905 an extension was opened from Hamilton to Larkhall and this view was taken that year in Union Street at Larkhall Cross. The line terminated in Church Street at John Street, which perhaps surprisingly is still known as "the terminus" to this day. The reason for this is probably unknown to many of the townsfolk, most of whom are no doubt unaware that until closure of the line in 1928 it was possible, albeit by changing at Cambuslang to the Glasgow system and at Dalmuir to the Dumbarton car to travel all the way to Balloch next to Loch Lomond by electric tram. On the left is car no. 9, one of the original fleet built in 1903 by the British Electric Car Co. of Trafford Park, Manchester, while no. 36 was new in 1905 and constructed by the Brush Electrical Engineering Co. of Loughborough.

Lanarkshire Tramways headquarters and depot were located at the Power House on Hamilton Road, Motherwell (after complete closure of the tramway system in 1931 it was re-named Traction House by Central SMT for their bus fleet). A short distance away was this attractive 18th century stone-arched bridge which spanned the Clyde to carry the main road between Hamilton and Motherwell until it was replaced in the early 1930s by the present Clyde Bridge. The tram line across the bridge was double tracked, unlike in many other areas where single track with passing loops sufficed. Two trams approach each other around 1910 on this busy section, the one on the left heading for Motherwell and carrying a full seated load on the open top deck. Advertising supplemented revenue for the tramway company and the left car displays a Heinz Baked Beans advert while the other features Van Houten's Cocoa.

New Stevenston, Tuesday August 1st, 1911 and an excited crowd of schoolboys and girls has gathered to witness the arrival and departure of the first electric tramcars to the village. On that day the Lanarkshire Tramways Co. extended its service on the projected Motherwell to Bellshill line from its previous terminus at Coursington Bridge over the River Calder. It was to be a further two years before the trams reached Bellshill and 1914 when the final section opened through to Uddingston where it met the Glasgow Corporation Tramways system. It is believed that this tram was no.50, one of seven built for Lanarkshire by the United Electric Car Co. of Preston in 1908. Disappointment, however, descended that August day on the assembled youngsters who had believed a rumour that the Tramways Co. would treat them to a free hurl. This was not to be.

The Monklands district also boasted its own tramway which commenced operation in February 1904 between Kirkwood Street, Langloan and Motherwell Street, Airdrie. The depot of the Airdrie & Coatbridge Tramways Co. was in Main Street, Coatbridge, near Jackson Street and this scene from the 1950s shows the interior when occupied by Standard cars 673 and 278 of Glasgow Corporation Tramways, who had taken over the Monklands system on January 1st 1922. The gap between the Langloan terminus and the Glasgow Corporation terminus at Baillieston was filled by new track extensions in 1923 and doubled by 1925 which allowed through running all the way from Airdrie to Ferguslie Mills on the former Paisley system, by this time also part of the GCT empire. Trams were nevertheless to be found in Coatbridge after Glasgow Corporation cut the service back to Baillieston in November 1956 as metal dealer James Connell of Locks Street purchased withdrawn cars for scrapping from both the Glasgow and Edinburgh systems as both municipalities had adopted a policy of tramway abandonment. Today Coatbridge is still home to trams as a variety of preserved examples operate at the Summerlee Museum in West Canal Street, providing the tram-riding experience to those too young to have travelled in the glory days.

The tram lines of Airdrie and Coatbridge were physically removed in 1959. This was Stirling Street Airdrie in April of that year, with Baxter's Leyland Royal Tiger HVA 883 passing the roadworks bound for Gartsherrie. James Baxter had started at Coatdyke in 1914 as a haulage contractor and charabanc proprietor. A network of local services in the Monklands towns was built up over the years and when the company sold out to Scottish Omnibuses in 1962 the fleet comprised 53 buses both single and double deck in an attractive bue and grey livery. From the mid 1950s Baxter's Bus Service was based at Gartlea Road Airdrie.

Airdrie Cross in the late 1940s, looking towards Coatbridge. Glasgow Corporation "Coronation" type tramcar no. 1185 heads for Langloan on the local shuttle service operated from Coatbridge depot which closed in November 1956 when the tram services were cut back to Baillieston. The SMT bus was an all Leyland Titan TD 5 which had been new in 1938, although appears older than the stylish tram, which was also new that year. BSC 533 was operating on the half-hourly service between Glasgow and Longriggend and would continue from Airdrie via Clarkston, Plains and Caldercruix. At this time the SMT livery was blue, prior to the re-adoption of green in 1949.

LOWER SALOON FRAME OF ALL-METAL
BUS BODY BY R. Y. PICKERING & CO. WISHAW.
NOTE: FULL LENGTH GIRDER & TRUSS PLATE
ALSO DIAGONAL BRACING

Opposite: One of the more prominent coachbuilding companies in Lanarkshire was Pickering of Wishaw which commenced business in the 1860s at their Netherton works and was perhaps best known for the construction of railway wagons, carriages and tram cars. Railway companies, not only in Britain but also overseas including South Africa and India, provided a good flow of business until the 1920s when this type of work took a downturn. For this reason Pickerings diversified and started to build bodywork for the bus industry which was on an upward swing at this time. Apart from many of the operators in the immediate Lanarkshire area, bus and tramcar bodies were built for major municipal fleets such as Glasgow, Edinburgh and Aberdeen Corporations. Other well-known major concerns which placed regular orders for Pickering bodywork included Central SMT in Motherwell, Young's Bus Service of Paisley, Lawson of Kirkintilloch, A1 Service of Ardrossan and AA Services of Ayr. Some of the larger English customers included Red & White of Chepstow, Northern General Transport, Gateshead and Hanson of Huddersfield. The final major order for buses was completed in 1950 for re-bodying AEC Regals for Northern General and Tynemouth & District. This side of the business was then discontinued, but contracts for railway wagons including major work for Pakistan Railways kept a fairly full workforce until 1960. The company was finally dissolved in 1987. The illustration shows the interior of Netherton works in 1939, with one of a fleet of 20 Albion Venturer double deckers built that year for Glasgow Corporation which became number 678 in the Glasgow fleet, registered CUS 843.

Nurserymen William Bryce & Sons of West End Nurseries, Carluke, featured in this testimonial advertisement which appeared in the commercial trade press during 1932. It extolled the virtues of Karrier commercial motor vehicles and in particular VA 3129, a 30cwt. model supplied to Bryce in 1924. Young's Window Company of Millbank Road, Wishaw, which supplied windows for all types of motor vehicle, was the Scottish agent for the Huddersfield-built Karrier chassis. The company founder, William Young, was at one stage Karrier's chief designer and accordingly quite a number were purchased by Lanarkshire firms.

Above, the vehicle is shown with a load of some 200 boxes of plants weighing over two tons, whilst the lower illustration depicts fifty cwts. of soil being removed from a field.

Here's Testimony

to the splendid record of a seven-year-old Karrier still giving wonderful service after covering well over 100,000 trouble-free miles.

WRITING with reference to the 30 cwt. Karrier delivered to them in 1924, Messrs. William Bryce & Sons, of West End Nurseries, Carluke, Scotland, state:

"Most people say a great deal if they get a poor machine, but we think they should also speak when the product does more than well. Our Karrier averages about 15,000 miles per year, and not once has it failed to complete a day's work . . . . . . Five years elapsed without a penny having to be spent on repairs; the engine bearings are still untouched, the gearbox and back axle have as yet to be opened up . . . . . . in fact, **a £10 note would cover the whole of our mechanical expense."**

RELY ON

"KARRIER"
Commercial Motor Vehicles

AND

SUCH SATISFACTION WILL BE YOURS!

From the days of the old horse drawn mail and stagecoaches, the main road south through Lanarkshire has echoed with generations of wheeled transport carrying passengers and goods to and from our neighbours over the border but surprising though it may seem it was not until the late 1920s that regular bus services were introduced on long distance cross border services. The main reason for this was that the incredibly low speed limit of only 12 m.p.h. was applied to commercial and passenger vehicles, despite the availability of reliable pneumatic tyres for some years previously. High mileage bus services were therefore simply not an option until 1928 when the limit was raised to a still unreasonably slow 20 m.p.h. From then many companies made the attempt to operate longer routes, including Lowland Motorways of Glasgow who introduced a service to Manchester, with an onward connection to London. This was the first regular road passenger service available between the cities since stagecoach days around 80 years previously, when the expanding railways had virtually killed the coach. This early 1930s scene shows GE 6001, a 1929 Leyland Tiger TS2 bodied by Pickering of Wishaw on the northbound Lowland service to Glasgow pausing for a refreshment halt at the Crawford Hotel, where in former years passengers would have arrived in considerably less comfort by stagecoach. The horses would have been changed prior to the long climb towards Beattock Summit on the southbound journey, while passengers on the north coach would be grateful that journey's end was not too far away. Also visible in this view is the bus from Dumfries to Biggar, West Linton and Edinburgh, operated by the Caledonian Omnibus Co. of Dumfries on the route which had recently been acquired with the business of Andrew Harper, Peebles.

James Harvie's first garage was situated in Abington when the village lay astride the old main A74 Carlisle Road, long before the bypass of the 1960s and therefore an ideal location for business. This animated late 1920s scene shows the original premises which were destroyed by fire in 1935 to be quickly replaced by another on the same site. Harvie came to Abington in 1890s and initially worked as a blacksmith and cycle dealer, later starting the garage for which he was granted AA accreditation. In the foreground is GD 4201, a Buick tourer new in 1926, while the diminutive car to the right with its hood down is SF 8472, a 1927 baby Austin. The Buick, although unmistakably an American car, was actually built at the company's Canadian factory for import to Britain, thus neatly avoiding the payment of punitive tax. David Buick, founder of the firm, was a Scotsman from Arbroath. Parked at the distant petrol pumps is a Great War Caledon lorry, distinguished by its fluted radiator and saltire badge, and registered SN 1171 in Dunbartonshire. This was built in Duke Street, Glasgow by Scottish Commercial Cars, which had initially held Scotland's Commer dealership, later constructing buses and lorries until a downturn in business hastened closure in 1926.

Brothers Robert, David and Bruce Dempster started business at this garage in Ayr Road, Larkhall in 1920 where they initially repaired bicycles, cars and farm machinery. Bruce is seen on the far right of this period scene while David's new Rudge-Multi motor cycle (GD 2409 of 1926) is seen to the left. Later they operated lorries which comprised Unic, Morris, Bedford, Dennis, Foden and Seddon over the years. Contract work to Lanarkshire County Council water and roads departments was undertaken and a milk collection service was developed around the local farms. Buses and coaches were also purchased including Lancia, Crossley, Dennis, Albion, Seddon and Bedford and apart from schools and private hire operations a summer weekend service was run from Hamilton to Blackpool in the 1960s and 1970s. Seen above is V 9843, one of two Lancia charabancs new in 1922 which could also serve as lorries when required as interchangeable bodies were available. In those early years a passenger service was operated between Netherburn, Larkhall and Hamilton but abandoned in the face of later opposition. Dempsters still own a garage in Larkhall today, in Burnhead Road.

A typical small town street scene in 1920s Lanarkshire. This view of Newmains in November 1928 shows Manse Road looking towards The Cross, with a dearth of motor vehicles in comparison with today's busy thoroughfare. Prominent in the foreground, parked beside the gas streetlamp is GD 331, a 1925 Morris Cowley which was William Morris's answer to the competition with Henry Ford's popular model T. This model of Morris was familiarly known as the "Bullnose" for obvious reasons. At the end of the tramtrack at Newmains Cross may just be seen two of the Lanarkshire Tramways Company cars (covered top and open top) at the terminus siding of the line from Wishaw and Cambusnethan, while a Glasgow General Omnibus Co. bus of A.E.C. manufacture sets out on its journey to the city. Although the buildings to the right of the street have now gone, the pharmacy on the extreme left remains in business as such to this day.

Mention the name Taggart around the Motherwell area and it will probably be associated with the well-known local garage rather than the TV detective series. James Taggart served his time as an engineer with Hurst, Nelson & Co., the tram and railway wagon builders in Motherwell, but started business for himself by opening a cycle shop in Brandon Street in 1897 at the very dawn of the then embryonic automobile. Natural development followed which by 1910 brought Taggart Bros. agencies for the Paisley-built Arrol-Johnston car and also the French Darracq. The above view is a glimpse inside the Knowetop premises in the late 1940s, shortly after the restrictions of World War 2. In the foreground is a mid-1930s Austin Six saloon carrying what today would be a valuable registration VA 77, issued originally in 1922. On the ramps is GM 3732, an Austin Ten of 1946. Demand for cars outstripped supply in the post-war years, giving Taggarts a ready sale for both second hand and new vehicles.

For over half a century the Central SMT Company, with headquarters at Traction House, Motherwell, provided the bulk of bus services throughout Lanarkshire. Hamilton boasted two Central depots, one in Burnbank Road, acquired with the business of J. W. & R. Torrance in 1932 and the other in Bothwell Road which had been the main depot of the Glasgow General Omnibus Co. (GOC) one of the largest constituent companies on the formation of Central in 1932. This mid 1950s scene shows the interior of the Bothwell Road premises, usually known as Clydesdale Garage, with a typical selection of Central buses of that time. Representing the large double deck fleet of Leyland Titans is L255 (CVA 355) of 1947 receiving attention from a mechanic. The others, from the left, are T63 (FV 5772) a Burlingham bodied Leyland Tiger TS7 of 1935 purchased from Leamington Tours of Blackpool and finished in Central's coach colours featuring a reversed application of their dark red and cream livery, T134 (AVA 375) a 1939 Alexander bodied Leyland Tiger TS8, K4 (DVD 704) a 1948 all-Guy Arab, T139 (AVA 380) another Alexander bodied Tiger of 1939 and T125 (VD 8776) a similar Tiger of 1938. As may be seen, Central favoured rear entrances on their single deckers.

SS 4050 was finished in the Brunswick green and cream fleet livery adopted by Hunter of Wishaw. This was an E.R.F. which had been supplied new in 1934 to Scottish agents Bowen of Edinburgh for the order of East Lothian contractor Andrew Hogg of Tranent. Numbered 15 with Hunter, it is seen on this occasion in the 1950s towing a trailer or "monkey" (known elsewhere as a "dolly") to accommodate a long steel drum from the Motherwell Bridge & Engineering Co. on a journey to a customer in the south of England. This early model E.R.F. (the first was produced in 1933, incorporating the famous Gardner engine long associated with this marque) was built by Edwin Richard Foden at his Sandbach factory in Cheshire. It gave sterling service and incredibly was not retired from Hunter's fleet until the early 1970s.

VS 2528 was a 3 ton Albion lorry supplied in 1934 to haulage contractor James Hogg of Cambuslang. The reason for the Greenock number rather than Lanarkshire was that the bodywork was constructed by Greenock based Albion agent and coachbuilder John Mitchell, who registered the vehicle prior to delivery. It carries the traditional Albion radiator, once so familiar in many transport fleets, with the rays of the rising sun embossed at the apex. The motto of Albion Motors was "Sure as the Sunrise", a maxim which every operator of Albions would agree was not an idle boast.

In addition to the bus services provided by Central SMT, by far the major operator in the county, Lanarkshire was home to a large number of privately owned bus companies, nonetheless important for the services they provided. These firms varied in size from single bus owners to much larger concerns such as the family owned Baxters of Airdrie, Laurie Bros.(Chieftain) of Hamilton, Carmichael (Highland) of Glenboig and Wilson of Carnwath. Jack McKnight of Wellgate, Lanark was one of the smaller operators and operated a Lanark local service. This view in the mid 1960s at New Lanark is from Long Row looking towards the 18th century New Buildings and the bell which once summoned the workers to the New Lanark mills. Smoke from the chimneys hangs in the air above the historic mill village, today restored and designated a World Heritage site. HWO 357 and 358 were two Duple-bodied Albion Valiant coaches of 1950 which McKnight purchased from Red & White Services of Chepstow, Monmouthshire.

Isaac Hutchison of Overtown was a former miner who started repairing motor cycles and cars shortly after the Great War before pioneering a passenger service initially with cars and then buses between Larkhall, Garrion Bridge, Overtown and Wishaw, later expanding to operate a wide variety of routes particularly to many of the Lanarkshire collieries carrying miners to and from their various shifts. Private hire work was also an important side of Hutchison's business and comfortable coaches always featured in the fleet, many with bodies built locally by Stewart's Coltness Coachworks. The firm was controlled by the Anderson family of Newhouse from 1960, developing further new services in the Motherwell and Wishaw area until 2007 when the business was sold to the transport giant First Bus, thus ending a long-lived and well-loved local company. This illustration from the era when "Hutchie" operated double deckers shows Leyland Titan PD2 KVA 511 of 1954 passing through Overtown bound for Larkhall on the service from Wishaw. This was one of the last Scottish-owned buses to be fitted with Leyland's own attractive bodywork as production ended that year to concentrate on truck cabs.

Daniel Henderson came to Carstairs in 1898 to be the village blacksmith at what was then a thatched smiddy. Like many others in that trade, horses were ousted by horse power as the motor age dawned and Daniel developed a garage business. After World War 2 buses and coaches including Bedford OBs, Albions and a Foden were operated mainly on schools and private hire duties but also on a country bus service by the back roads on Tuesdays and Saturdays between Biggar and Lanark, where former Chesterfield Leyland Tiger TS7c CRA 265 was photographed in 1957. In August, 1958 Henderson gave up the latterly uneconomic rural route which served such communities as Pettinain, Covington, Quothquan and Libberton. This Metro-Cammell bodied 32 seater with a delightful period piece oval rear window dated from 1936 and was initially fitted with torque convertor automatic transmission, later converted by Henderson to a manual gearbox. Lanark's Horsemarket bus stance had been used from the days of solid-tyred charabancs in the early 1920s and remained the town's bus terminal until the redevelopment of the area in the 1980s. Other companies to have used it over the years included Wilson's Gala motor transport to Forth and West Calder, Plenderleith's Tinto service to Symington and Biggar, Jackson's (later Whiteford's) to Auchenheath and Lesmahagow, Stoke's to Hawksland, Lesmahagow, Rigside and Coalburn, Leith's to Abington, Leadhills and Sanquhar, SMT to West Linton and Edinburgh and of course the variety of routes provided to and from Lanark by Central SMT. The fuel pump used by Central to replenish their buses can be seen in this view.

Peter Irvine & Sons of Muirhall Garage, Salsburgh, operated between Airdrie and Salsburgh on a service pioneered by Donald Munn of Harthill in the early 1920s. Irvine was also engaged in private coach hire using the fleet name Golden Eagle coaches which continues today although the stage service was given up in 1994. Exemplifying one of the coaches with Golden Eagle half a century ago, but still with a modern appearance, is OVD 795, a Leyland Tiger Cub with Duple bodywork, new to Irvine's in 1957.

An old established Lanarkshire haulage contractor and carrier was Ramage of Douglas Water, a firm which sadly ended business as recently as 2008. The fleet included FVD 409, an Albion Chieftain of 1950, finished in the company colours of light green with a red flash on the cab. The mining village was formerly home for two other hauliers, namely Richard Tinto and Mitchell Bros.

Another once familiar name, but now no longer seen in the county is that of the Clyde Alloy Steel Co. Ltd., Craigneuk Works, Motherwell, who supplied a wide range of rolled and cast alloy steels to industry. Their transport fleet in the 1950s included mainly Albions such as this, finished in the company's attractive livery of dark green with gold lettering.

Albion Claymore GM 8869 was new in 1957 to the well-known Wishaw confectionery makers King's Pure Sweets, alas no longer in business. I still recall schooldays when I'd savour the enjoyment of an Oddfellow as the very last drop of that unique fruity yet spicy flavour was sucked from the circular sweetie with that very individual cinnamon and clove taste made famous by King's. The underfloor-engined Claymore model was introduced by Albion Motors in 1954 and was described in contemporary advertising as having a "revolutionary new cab design giving a low, unobstructed floor and easy access". The body on this example in its blue and cream colours was built at John Stewart's Coltness coachworks, which was only a short distance along Kirk Road from the location of this view, photographed as the van delivered to local shops.

Yet another familiar name associated with the manufacture of sweet things is Thomas Tunnock of Uddingston. Still thriving in business today as bakers and confectioners, the firm's pedigree goes back as far as 1890, although their famous caramel wafers were not introduced until 1951. Horse drawn transport was initially provided but superseded by the well-known wee red vans, four of which are seen here on July 15, 1932 on the way to Uddingston cricket club with a major purvey. From the left are VD 497 of 1931, VA 8417 of 1929 and VA 7783 of 1928 (which were all Morris Commercials) and GG 7589, a Bedford of 1932.

Lanarkshire's VD registration mark was introduced in May 1930 when VA expired, having reached 9999. The three letter AVA mark did not appear until May 1938. VD 96 was a Leyland "Beaver" new in 1930 to the Coltness Iron Co. Ltd. of Newmains, seen being loaded with what appears to be a valve. This versatile company owned collieries not only in Lanarkshire (Branchal, Douglas, Duntilland, Hassockrigg, Kingshill, Overtown) but also in Fife and West Lothian which produced most types of household and steam coal and also anthracite and coal briquettes. Although their speciality was the manufacture of iron and steel castings especially for locomotives, other productions included Portland Cement (Caledonian brand), building bricks, fireclay products, limestone for both industrial and agricultural use and crushed slag for road making.

Virtually every co-operative society in Scotland had its own transport department, usually operating vans and lorries involved mainly in general collections and deliveries. Many societies owned mobile shops which travelled around housing schemes and outlying areas to reach customers who otherwise would perhaps find difficulty in reaching the town stores. Larkhall Co-operative Society Ltd. used this Commer Superpoise 3 tonner in the 1950s, seen outside the co-op grocery premises in Montgomery Street, now replaced by the Co-op funeral parlour.

The lorries of Coatbridge haulier William Nicol were easily recognisable in their post office red colours with cream relief. A varied fleet included A.E.C., Foden and Leyland chassis and here we see two of the Leylands. LVD 784 (fleet no. 43) was a 6-wheel Leyland Hippo while PFG 152 (no.59) was an 8-wheel Leyland Octopus, both dating from 1955. They are engaged on hauling steel tubes from the Imperial Tube Works, Coatbridge, a local company which provided Nicols with much of their work.

A 1962 view at Carnwath market square where the historic 16th century cross shows road distances on the shaft. Wilson's cream and red bus pauses before proceeding on the sparsely populated rural route from Forth to Edinburgh via Tarbrax and the former cattle drove road known as the Lang Whang traversing the lower slopes of the Pentland Hills. This is the somewhat bleak A70 road to the Capital. It was unusual to find the Fordson Thames chassis used for passenger work but this example was one of the exceptions. EFR 627 was a 1950 model with modernistic, for its time, coachwork by Bellhouse Hartwell of Westhoughton, Lancs. Owner Robert Wilson had started in the bus business as Gala Motor Transport in the early 1920s in Galashiels, moving to Biggar and then Whitelees, Lanark before basing the firm in Carnwath. In addition to various local services, Wilsons operated a large fleet of luxury coaches on private hire and tour work but the company ceased trading in 2001.

Although less robust than the heavier Albions, A.E.C.s and Leylands used by many of the larger haulage contractors, Ford commercial vehicles were nonetheless reliable and economic, in particular serving smaller hauliers well for their intended purposes. This was especially true of the three axle patented forward control versions converted to carry a greater payload. This specialised conversion was carried out for Scottish customers by main Ford dealer Alexander Motors of Semple Street, Edinburgh. A typical example was VD 498, supplied in 1931 to Andrew Hepburn of Coatbridge.

Leadhills, on the southernmost edge of the county, close to where Lanarkshire meets Dumfriesshire amongst the Lowther Hills. This tranquil scene shows the village in 1922, and remains largely unchanged today. The wheels visible to the right were then brand new. They belonged to V 9675, a Chevrolet open tourer which is parked outside Kerr's Hopetoun Arms Hotel, while on the other side of the street, adjacent to the hotel "motor garage" as described on the doors, is a two seat Morris Cowley "Bullnose." The county's initial motor licensing system used the single letter V, issued first in January 1904 followed by VA from July 1922 then VD from May 1930. Three letter combinations started with AVA in August 1938 then the suffix system in June 1964 with AVA-B. At the time of this photograph William Wallace of Leadhills ran a primitive bus to and from Lanark and to Sanquhar via the Mennock Pass and was based at the Hopetoun Arms garage, which had originally been a livery stable. In 1944 Wallace's business was acquired and continued by J. & J. Leith of Sanquhar, yet another firm which has ceased trading.

The Leadhills and Wanlockhead Railway was Britain's highest branch line, reaching almost 1500 feet above sea level. It was opened in 1901 by the Caledonian Railway Company from its main Glasgow to London line at Elvanfoot, specifically for transporting lead from the area to commercial markets, but in 1902 passenger trains were also introduced. The lead mines of Leadhills mainly closed in 1928 and those in neighbouring Wanlockhead (over the border into Dumfriesshire) in the 1930s, hastening the end of the railway, which closed to all traffic in January 1939. This Edwardian scene at Leadhills Station shows Caledonian 0-4-4 loco. No. 172 with a passenger train. As may be seen the station platform was at track level, requiring a fair degree of agility from the passengers to clamber in and out of the train.

Martin Anderson, or "Cynicus" was a well known Victorian artist, best known for his satirical cartoons. He started his own post-card publishing business in Tayport, Fife, in 1902 and in the example shown here, he pokes gentle fun at the Leadhills railway. In 1983 a society was formed to build and operate a 2 foot gauge tourist railway between Leadhills and Wanlockhead utilising the original trackbed. This is open to visitors during the summer months.

If you chance to come this way,
Take a trip to Elvanfoot
There, and back all in one day
Sure it is the fastest route

Annacker's Express to Leadhills

This sad scene shows the old main A 74 road near Abington looking north at Duneaton Bridge spanning Duneaton Water, a tributary of the Clyde. This was a fatal accident which killed driver Gordon McMillan and two passengers and took place on Tuesday August 30th 1938 when he was at the wheel of GG 9915, an A.E.C. 6-wheeler of 1933 owned by Youngs' Express Deliveries Ltd., of Paisley, whose main depot was in Portman Street, Glasgow. Fully laden with rolls of linoleum en route from Kirkcaldy to Manchester, Gordon lost control on the bend approaching the bridge and toppled to the water below. A member of Lanarkshire Constabulary, with twin-headed eagle cap badge, looks over the bridge while a Foden 6-wheeler approaches around the fateful bend. The old style tall telegraph poles marching into the distance are also noteworthy on a section of road which has been rendered almost obsolete by the dual carriageway of the M 74.

Owners of the luckless lorry on the previous page were Youngs' Express Deliveries Ltd., familiarly known as Y.E.D. This was a large concern with many depots, including one in Abington which had been built and previously occupied by livestock contractor Neil Black who had originally been based in Crawfordjohn. After nationalisation of Y.E.D. it became a British Road Services depot and today is occupied by haulier Reive Grossart. Amongst Youngs' lorries usually based at Abington were these three Scammell 8-wheelers in the green colours of the company, that on the right dating from 1940 while the others were 1938 models. All had Paisley (XS) registrations, signifying the Y.E.D. head office address. The line-up is pictured at Douglas Castle Lodge, now the site of Cairn Lodge service area at Happendon on the original A 74 road.

Hugh Clelland of Chryston was yet another haulage contractor who followed the pattern of having started business shortly after the Great War conducting collections and deliveries and furniture removals by horse and cart, progressing into the age of the motor lorry and expanding at the same time. Some of the many industrial companies for whom Clelland & Sons operated contracts included Caledonian Cement, Clyde Iron Works, Cardowan Fireclay, Clydebridge Steelworks, and Glenboig Brickworks. At its peak around 1970, a fleet of approximately 75 lorries and 120 trailers was operated amongst which were A.E.C., Atkinson, Bedford, Leyland, Maudslay, Mercedes, Scania and Volvo chassis and was accordingly one of the largest privately owned haulage concerns in Scotland. Sadly Hugh Clelland, son of the firm's founder, died in a tragic accident in 1971 and without his leadership the company was wound down and closed only a short time later. For several years the red-liveried fleet had favoured the Southall built A.E.C. and this scene shows VD 2663, a 1933 A.E.C. Matador and trailer delivering bagged cement at an unknown building site.

One of the final lorries to enter Clelland's Fleet before the business closed in the early 1970s was this Leyland Buffalo prime mover with Leyland's high datum ergonomic cab and fitted with their troublesome turbocharged 510 fixed head engine. GVA 955 K is seen in 1972 outside the former Newfield Inn on the main Airdrie to Cumbernauld road at Stand.

In addition to the Morton steam wagons and the Belhaven and Clyde vehicles built in the early years of the 20th century in Lanarkshire a further commercial vehicle manufacturer started production in 1970. This was the Argyle Motor Manufacturing Co. Ltd., based in Flakefield, East Kilbride which had no connection with the much earlier and differently spelled Argyll from Alexandria which also built cars and commercials. Named the Argyle "Christina", this was initially a 16 ton rigid chassis, soon followed by a short wheelbase 16 ton tipper, both featuring the Perkins 6 cylinder diesel engine with Eaton gearbox and 2 speed rear axle. Bodywork was built by Motor Panels of Coventry. Despite encouraging initial sales and good publicity the sturdy and reliable Argyle was unable to survive in a very competitive market and ceased production in 1973. Illustrated is the first Argyle Christina built, which was delivered in 1970 to Glasgow haulage contractor J. & R. Wright. Other customers included A. & J. Clark of Rutherglen, Robert Pollock of Maryhill and W.H. Malcolm of Brookfield.

For over half a century the name Sam Anderson has been synonymous with heavy haulage not only in Lanarkshire but in all corners of the country. Sam started as a bus driver for John Sword's Midland bus service of Airdrie, later becoming part of Western SMT. He bought his first lorry during World War 2 and quickly built up a sizeable fleet at his Newhouse base, mainly favouring AEC chassis in particular over the years until they were no longer available. This view from 1967 shows JVD 256 E, a Guy 'Big J' tractor unit hauling a trailer loaded with steel girders from Ravenscraig. The location is outside Sam Anderson's headquarters and main depot at Wilsons Road garage, between Newhouse and Hareshaw.

John Laurie of Hamilton commenced his transport business with a second hand model T Ford shortly after completing service in the 1914-18 war. Initially he carried miners to and from Hamilton Palace Colliery and developed the firm over the years by extending his services to cover Auldhouse, High Blantyre, East Kilbride (merely a village at the time) and Eaglesham. The fleetname Chieftain was adopted from the mid 1920s onwards and vehicle acquisitions between the wars included mainly Reo, Albion and Leyland makes, while during World War II examples of the wartime utility Bedford OWB type arrived. Post-war expansion for the company, which had been based at Burnbank since the mid 1930s, meant the arrival of more double deckers, including many second hand Daimlers and Leylands from Birmingham, Middlesborough and Sheffield Corporations and Leyland RTL types from London Transport. For new purchases the choice favoured Leyland Motors who supplied seven double deckers to Chieftain including two of the then newly introduced rear engined Atlantean models in 1960 and 1961. MVA 100, which was no. 55 in the dark green liveried fleet, is pictured shortly after entering service in 1955. This was a Leyland PD2/12 with lowbridge bodywork by Northern Counties of Wigan and is seen in the infant new town of East Kilbride, then bereft of traffic, on the route between Hamilton and Hairmyres Hospital. When the Chieftain business was sold to Central SMT in 1961, thirty-one buses passed to their new owner including MVA, which became L206 with Central, operating mainly from their East Kilbride depot until 1969 when it passed to Highland Omnibuses in Inverness for further service as their JD8.

STIRLING'S MOTOR CARRIAGES, Ltd.,
HAMILTON, N.B.
THE PIONEERS OF THE SCOTTISH MOTOR INDUSTRY.

Highest Awards AT **London Shows,** 1899.

Highest Awards AT **London Shows,** 1899.

MAKERS OF ALL KINDS OF MOTOR CARRIAGES.

Broughams, Family 'Buses, Stanhopes, Dog Carts, Waggonettes, etc., fitted with the well known **DAIMLER MOTORS.** Fitted with **PENNINGTON MOTORS:**—Victoria de Luxe Mail Car, Sociable, Universal Car, Medical Brougham, Hansom, Delivery Van, etc.

Steam Omnibuses and Steam Waggons, 1 to 4 tons. Motor Tricycles and Quadricycles of every description.

☞ *EXPERT ADVICE GIVEN.* *DRIVING TAUGHT.* 🐟

A contemporary advert of October 1899 from the 'Motor Car World', one of the very few motoring publications available in those pioneering days when cars were still in their infancy. John Stirling of Hamilton (page 2) not only built the bodywork on a variety of early motor vehicles but also operated what were almost certainly the first motorised public transport services in Lanarkshire. These commenced in October 1897 with 8 seat solid tyred Daimler 4 h.p wagonettes on routes from Hamilton to Larkhall and Hamilton to Blantyre and Uddingston, under the name Scottish Motor Omnibus and Car Co. Ltd. Hamilton. The vehicle shown in the advert was an 18 seat Leyland steam bus bodied by Stirling and supplied to the Dundee and District Tramways Co. Ltd. in June 1899. This is of particular interest as it was probably the first passenger vehicle built by the Lancashire Steam Motor Co., predecessor of Leyland Motors.